Sonia Allison
MAKING GIFTS WITH FOOD

DAVID & CHARLES
Newton Abbot   London   North Pomfret (Vt)

British Library Cataloguing in Publication Data

Allison, Sonia
  Making gifts with food.
  1. Cookery   2. Entertaining
  I. Title
  641.5'68   TX739

  ISBN 0-7153-8264-0

© Sonia Allison 1982

All rights reserved. No part of this
publication may be reproduced, stored
in a retrieval system, or transmitted,
in any form or by any means, electronic,
mechanical, photocopying, recording or
otherwise, without the prior permission
of David & Charles (Publishers) Limited

Typeset by Typesetters (Birmingham) Limited,
Edgbaston Road, Smethwick, Warley,
West Midlands
and printed in Great Britain
by A. Wheaton & Co, Hennock Road, Exeter
for David & Charles (Publishers) Limited
Brunel House   Newton Abbot   Devon

Published in the United States of America
by David & Charles Inc
North Pomfret   Vermont 05053 USA

Contents

1	Making the Most of Your Gifts	4
2	Cooking Kits	9
3	Pâtés and Spreads	12
4	Dressings, Sauces, Relishes, Butters	18
5	Preserves – Jams and Chutneys	27
6	Cakes	34
7	Puddings	46
8	Biscuits	50
9	Confectionery	57
10	Food Hampers, Fruit and Nuts	62

1
Making the Most of Your Gifts

Everyone welcomes a homemade gift that is both good to eat or use and handsomely presented, and the aim of this little book is to suggest to you some of the more popular 'make-to-give-away' sweet and savoury specialities that are popular with all age groups. Their appearance is as important as their taste: so here too are ideas on how to pretty them up with the right kind of packaging. For instance, a foil-lined, once-used, sturdy chocolate-box with a doily lining, and cling film or cellophane cover, looks much more inviting than a mere paper bag for fudge or truffles; a circular or square tin, perhaps one that originally held tea or biscuits, covered with bright felt or floral wallpaper then edged with braid or ribbon, makes a splendid home for sweets, nuts or even do-it-yourself muesli.

Presentation can make or mar all your efforts, so below are some general suggestions which should add a professional touch to your gift-giving, at the same time providing you with a little light-hearted fun and the opportunity of testing out your own creative talents. Directions for packing are also given with the recipes.

Glasses
Small tumblers and wine-type stemmed glasses make excellent containers for hard butter sauces (such as rum or brandy butters), savoury butters and assorted spreads. Top-quality glasses are unnecessary; I have bought all

sorts of interesting shapes and colours in supermarkets, from white-elephant stalls at jumble sales, and also from antique shops and fairs where really lovely oddments are often sold off at low cost.

Jars

Always useful for mayonnaise, jams, marmalades, pickles and chutneys. Even the plainest of the plain jars can be dressed up. Try covering them with cling film, then overwrapping with a piece of gingham or other printed fabric, tied round with ribbon or string. Add a decorative label describing the contents.

Fancy Moulds and Cake Tins

Again, look round junk stalls for some oldies or simply buy fancy-shaped metal moulds and cake tins (fluted ones make super containers) and lacquer with gloss paint, allowing plenty of time to dry. Fill with chocolates, sweets, truffles, biscuits, nuts, etc, first put into polythene bags. Alternatively, line moulds or cake tins with foil, fill with whatever you like and cover with cling film so that contents show through. Secure with Sellotape if necessary and decorate top with a large bow of ribbon or artificial flower; a floppy poppy looks attractive and glittery flowers are appropriate for Christmas. Old jelly moulds, in thick glass, make original containers and look most attractive if packed with brightly-wrapped sweets and chocolates. They should be covered with cling film in the same way as the moulds or tins and can also be decorated with flowers and ribbon.

Plates, Platters and Dishes

Stemmed cake stands (new or secondhand), oval dishes, round or oblong plates and both shallow and deep dishes are worth buying as 'holders' for large and small cakes, fancy breads, biscuits, fresh fruit (instead of baskets), pâtés, and to make up the unusual cooking kits – Chinese, Swiss, Indian, Italian, French and Spanish, described in the next chapter. Those bits and pieces left over from tea or dinner services which just sit in a cupboard taking up space can also be used.

Mugs, Beakers and Pottery Containers

Personalised mugs and beakers decorated with names of your family and friends, or pets and cartoon characters, always make a welcome gift, packed with sweets, biscuits, nuts, fancy teas and coffees and even things such as breakfast-cereal mixes and bouquet-garni bags. Cover as directed for jars, using either cling film or foil, and add decorations to suit the season or person. Pottery containers are ideal for sweet and savoury butters and small amounts of rich pâtés. If time permits, collect different kinds of mugs and so on when on holiday abroad; and look around Britain too, as most counties have small, individual potteries which offer original designs. The skill here is to give yourself plenty of time to go hunting about and buy whenever you find something unusual and appropriate.

Tea and Coffee Pots

Silver-plated tea and coffee pots, from the turn of the century, can often be found at secondhand shops and antique fairs and even if imperfect, still make fairly inexpensive and practical containers for blends of tea and coffee. They are especially appreciated by friends in other parts of Europe, and in the USA, who welcome British antiques with unfailing enthusiasm. Pottery or bone-china versions are also highly acceptable and here there is ample opportunity to match the design and colouring to the person. Perhaps tie a card, with this piece of advice attached, to the teapot: 'Once empty, open the lid, half-fill the pot with water and use as a vase for small flowers.'

Boxes

Plain boxes are very useful for layers of biscuits with tissue paper between and, if shallow enough, for homemade sweets (in paper cases) in a single layer. The lid can be covered with a 'montage' of old Christmas-card fronts if the gift is intended for Christmas, and the sides covered with foil. Alternatively, the box and lid can be covered in fancy paper, carefully glued in place, and the inside lined with doilies or a small linen or cotton table napkin or pretty handkerchief.

Tins

Tins are useful for packaging all manner of foods: here are a few ideas for decoration.

1 Brush the outside with glue and cover with velvet cut to fit. Camouflage the fabric join with fancy braid (the kind used for trimming lampshades), then add bands of

braid to top and lower edges, securing with more glue.

2 Brush the outside with glue and cover with bright material. Dot material with more glue, then cover with white or coffee-coloured lace. Cover joins and top and lower edges with satin-faced or velvet ribbon, and hold in place with more glue.

3 Brush a round, shallowish tin with glue, then cover with felt or velvet. Stick on trimmings of gold braid to resemble a drum. If tin is square, glue on black felt and stick on rounds of white felt to make it look like a dice.

4 Cover with flowered vinyl, securing it in place with glue unless it is self-adhesive. Decorate join and lower edge with ribbon or braid then add a gathered frill of wider ribbon or broderie anglaise to top edge.

Note: Once the tins are decorated as described above, the lids will not fit. Therefore the contents should be covered for protection with cellophane paper or cling film.

Baskets
With so many sizes and shapes readily available and inexpensively priced, fresh fruit and nuts can be artistically arranged as you like, be it one bunch of grapes in a baby basket or a whole selection of seasonal fruits for a very special person. And instead of paying the earth for a Christmas food hamper, why not make your own? Use a Dundee or iced fruit cake as the centre-piece and surround it with cans and packets of seasonal foods, plus homemade sweets and other kitchen-prepared goodies. A bow of ribbon tied on the handle should complete the picture, with a cover of cellophane paper secured with Sellotape. If you have saved some of the smaller, slatted baskets used for strawberries and other soft fruits, paint with bright emulsion, line with a contrasting handkerchief and fill with sweets and small biscuits.

Swag-bags and Sacks
These can easily be made at home from pieces of hessian. Cut them into oblongs, then fold these in half and stitch, by hand or machine, along both long edges. The top should be hemmed and the bag or sack turned inside out. Cord threaded through the hemmed part will make a sack if pulled and knotted; for the swag-bag, all you have to do is to draw the top together and tie round

underneath with ribbon or cord. Fill the bags with anything you like from biscuits to nuts; this makes an unusual way of packaging. The bags or sacks themselves can be decorated with cut-out shapes made from felt or cardboard and glued to the outside. Or make bags from any suitable pieces of decorative material, perhaps with contrasting cord, braid or ribbon.

Tea-towels
Tea-towels, in cheerful designs and colours, make marvellous wrappings. They are particularly well-suited to cakes (which should first be protected with foil or cling film) and, if tied round with ribbon, look like miniature packages.

Accessories
Keep the following handy:

Assorted ribbons, cord and string
Artificial flowers and fruits
Pretty and decorative labels
Cake frills
Paper cases for sweets and cakes
Cling film
Foil
Materials for covering jars, such as gingham, flower-printed cotton, felt, etc
Braids
Sellotape
Glue
Tissue paper in assorted colours

2
Cooking Kits

This is a way to please all your friends with their favourite foods and makes a more personalised gift than most.

Indian
Choose Assorted curry powders in tins, 1 or 2 jars of chutney, packet of Basmati rice, packet of 'fry-them-yourself' poppadoms, tin and packet of Indian tea and a paperback book on Indian cooking.

Packing Arrange in a shallow round basket lined with Indian printed fabric. (For this you can cut up an old skirt or top, or even use a printed silk or cotton scarf.) Wrap completely in cling film.

Chinese
Choose A selection of Chinese condiments such as ready-prepared sweet-sour sauce and soy sauce plus rice wine or medium sherry. Include also some Chinese-style noodles, tin each of lychees and mandarins, packet of chopsticks, packet of China tea, some incense sticks and a paperback book on Chinese cooking.

Packing Arrange in a metal wok or on a round or oblong plate with an Oriental design. Wrap in cling film.

Italian

Choose Bottle or can of olive oil, can of anchovies in oil, large can of tomatoes, jar of black olives, 4oz (125g) piece of Parmesan cheese or tub of grated, medium-sized salami, packet each of spaghetti, ribbon noodles and lasagne, jar each of grated nutmeg, garlic granules, dried basil and marjoram, packet of bay leaves, bottle of Marsala and tin or tube of tomato purée. Include also recipes for making Spaghetti Bolognese, Lasagne and Pizza.

Packing Arrange in a shallow basket, in a large Italian pottery flower-pot or in a medium-sized wooden tub. Wrap in cellophane or cling film and tie on a miniature bottle of Strega, a typical Italian liqueur. As an alternative, buy a large pizza tin and use as a base for the foods.

French

Choose Packet of bouquet-garni bags, an assortment of French mustards, bottle or can of walnut and/or olive oil, jars of dried tarragon, rosemary and thyme, can or tube of tomato purée, bottle of wine vinegar, small bottle of cognac, packet of bay leaves, jar of real egg mayonnaise and small box of glacé fruits or marrons glacés.

Packing Line a handled basket with a check tea-towel and fill with the ingredients. Cover with a second tea-towel. Tie a miniature bottle of Grand Marnier to the handle.

Spanish

Choose Bottle of Rioja wine, miniature bottle of brandy and a large can of fruit cocktail to make Sangria. For Paella: large packet of long-grain rice, jar of saffron strands, jar of stuffed olives, head of garlic, bottle or can of olive oil, can of tomatoes. Add neatly written cards with directions and ingredients for both recipes (easy to find in the numerous foreign cook books on the market).

Packing Arrange on a large oval platter or in a paella pan (available from some major department stores and kitchen boutiques). Wrap in cling film and decorate with red fringing and an artificial red or pink carnation.

As an alternative Pad out a large, shallow box with some coloured tissue paper and fill with a bottle of sherry and 6 or 12 sherry glasses, depending on how generous you feel. Wrap in coloured cellophane. If liked, include a book on sherry.

Swiss

Choose A selection of Swiss Cheeses (preferably pre-wrapped), head of garlic, bottle of Swiss wine, 4 or 8 fondue forks. You can include jars of picked onions, olives and gherkins if you like, as these are often served with a traditional fondue.

Packing Stack into a fondue pot and wrap in cling film. Tie on a miniature bottle of kirsch. If the fondue pot is too expensive, choose a chunky pottery dish or bowl and line it with a straw or raffia mat to give the whole thing a rustic appearance. Tie on the kirsch with ribbon. Remember to include full instructions on the making of a Swiss fondue.

3
Pâtés and Spreads

Pâtés and sweet or savoury spreads are always useful as small gifts to take to family and friends when visiting. The children could make the easier spreads and pack them as they will — many children are instinctively creative and come up with attractive surprises.

Smoked Haddock Pâté

A particular treat, this one, which I am sure will be valued by those who enjoy something a little different. Make one day for the next where possible, though the pâté does store quite well for about 4 days. You do need a blender or food processor for this one.

8oz (225g) cooked and flaked smoked haddock (cooked weight *without* skin and bones)
1 garlic clove

2oz (50g) butter (please *not* margarine)
1/4 tsp white pepper
3 tsp fresh lemon juice
1-2oz (25-50g) extra butter (optional)

1 Place all ingredients (except extra butter) into blender goblet or food processor. Run the machine until mixture forms a smooth pâté.
2 Spoon smoothly into a smallish glass or china soufflé dish or pottery dish. If liked (and to form a good seal),

pour extra melted butter over the top which will set in a hard layer when cold.
3 Cover with cling film and store in the refrigerator until ready for packing.

Packing Cover top with piece of gingham or Laura Ashley-type floral print. Tie round with string. Add a decorative label describing contents. Stand in a box lined with tissue paper. Wrap in cellophane paper.

French-style Blender Pâté

A more sophisticated pâté in which the tin is lined with bacon rashers. Make only 2 days ahead of time and keep the recipe up your sleeve for an occasion when a friend is making an informal party and asks all the guests to bring some food with them. It makes a super contribution.

6 long rashers streaky bacon (about 12oz or 350g), de-rinded
1lb (450g) frozen chicken livers (thawed if frozen)
1 garlic clove, peeled and sliced
6oz (175g) onions, peeled and sliced
3oz (75g) butter or margarine
1½oz (40g) flour
½pt (275ml) cold milk
1 level tsp salt
¼ level tsp allspice
1 tsp Worcester sauce
freshly ground black or white pepper
6 small bay leaves

1 'Stretch' bacon rashers by standing between two sheets of greaseproof paper and rolling with a rolling-pin. Use to line a 1½pt (840ml) well-greased oblong loaf tin.
2 Fry livers, garlic and onions slowly in 2oz (50g) butter or margarine until they turn light golden-brown and the onions are just beginning to soften. Leave on one side for time being.
3 To make sauce, melt rest of butter or margarine in pan and stand over medium heat. Stir in flour to form roux. Cook for 2 minutes without browning.
4 Gradually blend in milk. Cook, stirring, until sauce thickens. Simmer for 2 minutes. Season with salt, allspice, Worcester sauce and pepper.
5 Blend livers, garlic and onions with the sauce in blender goblet until just smooth. Spoon evenly into bacon-lined tin and arrange bay leaves over the top. Cover with buttered foil.
6 Stand in roasting tin containing 1in (2.5cm) warm water which acts as a water bath or *bain marie*. Place in

oven preheated to 180°C (350°F), Gas 4.
7 Cook for 1¼ hours. Remove from oven and cool. Uncover, take off the bay leaves and discard. Turn pâté out onto board. When completely cold, transfer to decorative oblong or oval plate. Cover completely with cling film. Store in the refrigerator until ready for packing.

Packing Stand plate of covered pâté in a box or basket and pad round edges with a couple of pretty tea-towels. Add a little card saying the pâté should be sliced before serving and accompanied by hot toast.

Norwegian Liver Pâté

A marvellous pâté – sometimes called paste in Scandinavia – which I make all the year round with those tubs of frozen chicken livers now readily available from supermarkets. Sometimes I mix chicken and ox liver for a stronger flavour. The pâté turns out like a firm loaf, is very easy to slice and makes an appetizing starter with hot toast, a delicious main course with salad or even hot vegetables, and a welcome sandwich filling. It keeps up to one week in the refrigerator.

- 1lb (450g) chicken livers, thawed if frozen (or use half chicken and half ox liver)
- 3oz (75g) onion, peeled and chopped
- 2oz (50g) plain flour
- 2oz (50g) butter or margarine, melted
- 1 egg (size 2), beaten
- ¼pt (150ml) whipping cream, fresh milk or unsweetened evaporated milk
- 1 tbsp brandy or dry sherry
- ¼ level tsp allspice
- ¼ level tsp nutmeg (optional)
- ¼ level tsp white pepper (optional)

1 Well grease a 2lb (1kg) oblong loaf tin and line base and sides with aluminium foil or Bakewell non-stick parchment paper. Set oven to 180°C (350°F), Gas 4.
2 Mince chicken livers (or mixture of livers) with onion directly into bowl. Stir in flour, butter or margarine, egg, cream or one of the milks, brandy or sherry, allspice, nutmeg and pepper if used.
3 The mixture will be very soft at this stage but will solidify during baking. Cover top of tin with greased foil then bake for 2 hours.
4 Remove from oven and uncover. Turn out of tin when cold. Remove lining paper. Wrap pâté in cling film.

Packing Wrap in foil then stand on a wooden board and put into an attractive box with a packet of ready-prepared toast. Cover with cellophane or other fancy paper. Alternatively, tie in a rustic-looking tea-towel and place in an oblong basket with a handle.

Greek Taramasalata

This is what I term the 'al fresco' pâté which is more like a dip but a great favourite with the young-at-heart, and is relatively good-natured in that it keeps at least a week to a week-and-a-half in the refrigerator. This is another recipe that needs a blender or food processor.

3oz (75g) jar of smoked cod roe or 6oz (175g) in the piece, both available from delicatessens, speciality shops, food or fish markets
2 large slices of white bread, cubed with crusts left on
1 garlic clove, peeled and sliced
4 tbsp salad oil
juice of one medium lemon
6-8 tbsp hot water
freshly ground white pepper to taste

1 If using roe from a jar, spoon straight into blender goblet or food processor. If using the kind of roe which comes as a whole piece, scrape it away from the skin before putting it into the goblet or food processor.
2 Add bread cubes, garlic, salad oil, lemon juice and half the hot water.
3 Run machine until mixture is smooth, adding more water until the mixture takes on the consistency of a thick, very pale pink mayonnaise. Season with pepper.

Do not coat top with melted butter but cover with cling film. Leave in the refrigerator until ready for packing.

Packing Pack as directed for the Smoked Haddock Pâté. If liked, add a small Greek cookbook to the box for a special gift. Or even a guidebook to Greece.

Dutch Chocolate Spread

4 level tbsp cocoa powder
2oz (50g) Dutch butter, softened
½ tsp vanilla essence
1 level tbsp pure cane syrup or black treacle
2 level tbsp sweetened condensed milk

1 Sift cocoa powder into bowl. Add butter, vanilla, syrup or treacle and milk.
2 Beat all ingredients together until smooth and evenly mixed and no streakiness remains. Pack straight away, as the spread firms-up on standing.

Packing Pack into a small glass (see Chapter 1) such as a whisky tumbler, then cover securely with cling film. Wrap top in chocolate-coloured fabric and tie round with contrasting ribbon, fancy string, narrow braid, etc. Attach a label with name of contents. For an alternative container, use a chunky pottery container. Wrap as directed and tie label to the handle.

TIP: Chocolate spread is suitable for spreading on semi-sweet breads, halved buns and fairly plain biscuits. It keeps up to one month in the refrigerator so can be prepared well ahead of time.

Curry Spread

An unusual spread and very appetizing on hot toast or crumpets — but it is fairly hot, so reserve for curry enthusiasts. Keeps in the refrigerator for up to a week.

2oz (50g) butter, softened
3 level tsp fine semolina
1 rounded tsp chunky peanut butter
2 level tbsp mild curry powder
1 level tsp Marmite
½ level tsp golden syrup
finely grated peel and juice of one small lemon

1 Cream butter until soft then beat in rest of ingredients.
2 When smooth and evenly combined, pack as suggested for Cheese and Mackerel Spread.

Cheese and Mackerel Spread

This is best made in a blender or food processor and should be prepared the day before giving.

8oz (225g) smoked mackerel fillets, skin and bones removed and the flesh coarsely flaked
2oz (50g) butter or margarine, softened
1oz (25g) Cheddar cheese, finely grated
3 tsp lemon juice
½ tsp Worcester sauce
½ tsp creamed horseradish or horseradish sauce

1 Place all ingredients into blender goblet or food processor. Run machine until smooth.
2 Pack straight away, as spread firms-up on standing.

Packing Spoon into attractive glass or pottery pot, making sure mixture reaches to the top. Cover with cling film or foil. Wrap top in squares of gingham (or other patterned material), then tie with string. Add a blob of red sealing-wax to knot and a decorative label with the name of the spread.

Cheese Spread

This is an appetizing spread for sandwiches, hot toast, scones and even waffles. Make no more than two days in advance.

3oz (75g) butter, softened
8oz (225g) firm cheese (such as Cheddar or Edam), finely grated
1 level tsp prepared English or continental mustard
1 tsp Worcester sauce
white pepper to taste

1 Cream butter until very light then gradually beat in cheese and rest of ingredients.
2 Pack straight away as spread firms-up on standing.

Packing Smooth evenly into a small pottery dish with lid and, if possible, choose brown stoneware. Seal lid to dish with Sellotape, then pack into a box. Wrap in suitable paper, then tie with ribbon, string or braid.

Cheese and Nut Spread

Make up Cheese Spread as directed. Then add 1oz (25g) chopped and salted peanuts with rest of ingredients. Pack as for Cheese Spread.

4
Dressings, Sauces, Relishes, Butters

Useful gifts for all seasons and easy to make and to pack. Dressings based on soured cream or cream cheese should be prepared the day before, and stored in the refrigerator overnight. Avoid putting any of the dressings into jars with metal lids.

Brandy or Rum Butter (also called Hard Sauce) to go with a Christmas Pudding, or a jar of Mint or Apple Sauce for a joint, will be warmly accepted and used with pleasure. Few such recipes take long to make, but please note that those based on butter obviously have a limited lifespan and should be kept in the refrigerator before giving away.

French Dressing *(for green and mixed salads)*

- 8 tbsp salad oil
- 1 level tsp powdered mustard
- 1/2 level tsp salt
- 1/2 level tsp caster sugar
- 1/2 level tsp Worcester sauce
- 1/4 level tsp white pepper
- 4 tbsp malt vinegar or lemon juice (or 2 tbsp of each)

1 Beat oil with mustard, salt, sugar, Worcester sauce and pepper.

2 Whisk in vinegar or lemon juice (or mixture). Transfer to suitable container (see below).

Packing Pour into any attractive jar or bottle with a stopper. A chemist may be obliging and sell you some medicine bottles with fitting corks. Alternatively, buy a mixed selection of corks to suit assorted bottles you may have in stock; shops selling wine-making kits are good places to go, or shops specialising in kitchen ware. Add a decorative label to each bottle, describing contents, then wrap in fancy paper as though you were wrapping a wine bottle. If preferred, wrap in sacking or hessian and tie round the top with string.

Blue Cheese Dressing *(for green and mixed salads. Also salads with eggs)*

Follow recipe and method for French Dressing but *before* you start, mash 1oz (25g) blue cheese in a small basin, then beat in all remaining ingredients in order given.

Packing As French Dressing.

Italian Anchovy and Herb Dressing *(for all green and mixed salads)*

Follow recipe and method for French Dressing but beat in, at very end, 1 level tsp anchovy essence, 2 rounded tbsp chopped parsley, 1 rounded tbsp drained and chopped capers, and 1 peeled and crushed garlic clove.

Packing As French Dressing.

Garlic Dressing *(for all green and mixed salads)*

Follow recipe and method for French Dressing, but add one peeled and sliced garlic clove at the end.

Packing   As French Dressing.

Yogurt Dressing

This is a good keeper and is especially suited for serving over fresh fruit salads, making a change from cream.

1 carton (5oz or 142ml) natural yogurt	1 tbsp fresh lemon juice
juice of one medium sweet orange	3 tsp melted golden syrup
	½ level tsp finely grated orange peel

1 Beat all ingredients well together.
2 Cover with cling film and store in the refrigerator until ready for packing.

Packing   Spoon neatly into a small glass jar. Cover with cling film, then wrap top in a square of brightly-coloured fabric, preferably one patterned with fruits. Stand in a box and add a card with your own favourite fruit-salad recipe. Top box with lid if it fits. Alternatively cover with cellophane paper.

Soured-cream Mustard Dressing

Particularly good over exotic-style mixed vegetable salads or as a cold sauce with hot roast beef.

1 carton (5oz or 142ml) soured cream	1 level tsp prepared English or continental mustard
½ level tsp onion salt	½ tsp Worcester sauce
	salt and pepper to taste

1 Beat soured cream smoothly with onion salt, mustard and Worcester sauce. Season with salt and pepper.
2 Cover. Refrigerate no longer than 24 hours before packing and giving away.

Packing   Spoon into a small pottery mug with handle. Cover with cling film. Attach a card to the handle with ribbon or thick thread, emphasising that the dressing must be kept in the refrigerator for no longer than 24 hours. Serving suggestions, written on the same card, might be helpful.

Gooseberry Sauce

Almost forgotten with the passing of time but once a very popular sauce indeed which, when served with mackerel, duck and goose, delighted the palate with its unusual tang and colour. It deserves to be reborn and is well worth considering if you have more garden gooseberries than you know what to do with.

8oz (225g) washed green gooseberries, topped and tailed
3 tbsp water
½ level tsp very finely grated lemon peel

2oz (50g) granulated sugar (or less if you like a sharper sauce)
1 rounded tsp butter or margarine

1 Tip gooseberries into pan with water and lemon peel. Simmer, covered, until fruit is very soft and pulpy.
2 Add sugar with butter or margarine. Stir over low heat until melted. Cool completely in saucepan.

Packing Pack in glass jars, tumblers or small dishes, cover tops with cling film and sunshine-yellow or leaf-green fabric, tied round with white ribbon.

Horseradish Sauce

A beauty for roast beef and smoked trout, but make only 1 day in advance, because unlike commercial varieties this recipe will not keep long. In any case, store in the refrigerator until ready for packing.

1 carton (¼pt or 142ml) soured cream
2 tbsp cold milk
3 tbsp white vinegar (colourless)

1½-2 level tbsp grated horseradish (available prepared in jars)
1 level tsp caster sugar
salt and pepper to taste

1 Mix cream with milk, vinegar, grated horseradish and sugar.
2 Season to taste with salt and pepper, then cover closely with cling film. Store in the refrigerator until ready for packing.

Packing Spoon into a small pottery jar with a rustic design. Cover first with cling film and then with foil. Tie round with coloured string and attach a label describing contents.

Mint Sauce

A thoughtful gesture on your part would be to take some Mint Sauce with you if you know your host or hostess will be serving lamb. Use fresh garden mint for this recipe and not the bottled kind.

8 rounded tbsp very finely chopped mint leaves
1 level tbsp caster sugar
2 tbsp boiling water
4 tbsp malt vinegar

1 Tip mint into small bowl. Dissolve sugar in the boiling water.
2 Add to mint with vinegar. Cool completely.

Packing Transfer to a decorative jar, cover securely with cling film (allowing it to come one-third of the way down the jar), then add a well-fitting lid. Attach a coloured label with description of contents.

Sweetcorn and Pepper Relish with Carrots

An unusual, sweet-and-sour relish for meat and poultry roasts, and rather special with barbecued foods. It needs about five days in the refrigerator to mature.

4oz (125g) caster sugar
½ level tsp salt
1 level tsp prepared mild mustard
¼pt (150ml) malt vinegar
about 4 drops Tabasco sauce
1lb (450g) frozen sweetcorn, cooked and drained
4oz (125g) carrots, peeled and very finely grated
1 small red pepper
1 small green pepper
2oz (50g) onion, peeled and finely grated

1 Put sugar, salt, mustard, vinegar and Tabasco into a saucepan. Stir over low heat until sugar dissolves.
2 Bring to the boil and cover. Lower heat slightly. Boil for 2 minutes. Stir in sweetcorn and carrots. Turn off heat.
3 Halve both peppers and remove seeds. Cut flesh into strips then chop coarsely. Cover with boiling water and leave to stand for 1 minute to soften slightly.
4 Drain. Add peppers to corn mixture with the onion. Mix thoroughly. Cool completely in the pan.
5 Tip into a bowl, cover with cling film and leave in the refrigerator until ready for packing.

Packing Spoon into any decorative glass container, even an old glass jelly mould. Cover with cling film, then wrap top in either fancy paper or patterned aluminium foil (available at Christmas time for gift wrapping). Attach a label to each container describing contents, and also tie on a card with serving or using suggestions.

Savoury Butters

Whether spread in between slit French bread (cut into slices almost to base and wrapped in foil), and later warmed through in the oven and served with soups or stews, or dolloped onto freshly-baked jacket potatoes, or served in pats as a garnish on grills of meat, poultry or fish, Savoury Butters contribute their own special flavour and a note of distinction to a dish. They are essentially 'hard' savoury sauces which melt into and onto foods, providing moisture and succulence in luxurious way.

After shaping and packing, all the Savoury Butters should be stored in the refrigerator (up to one week) or freezer (up to two months) until ready to give away. Use unsalted butter or your final dish may be oversalted.

Anchovy Butter *(for fish and veal grills)*

4oz (125g) unsalted butter, soft but not runny	3-4 level tsp anchovy essence 1 tsp lemon juice

1 Beat butter to a smooth cream, then add anchovy essence and lemon juice.
2 Continue to beat until well mixed. Pack straight away.

Packing Spoon evenly into small coffee cups (oddments left over from sets, or picked up on a market stall are fun) and stand on matching saucers. Attach a label describing contents and also a gift card saying what each is for, and how to use. Cover with cling film, then wrap completely with more cling film, so enclosing cup and saucer. Alternatively, spoon Butters into chunky pottery pots (the sort one often finds in French bistros or Italian trattorias), label and cover with cling film. Box 3 or 4 together, then top with lid if it fits, or alternatively wrap in attractive paper. For a special present, you could add an unusual, secondhand butter knife from Victorian or Edwardian days or a modern one with a wooden or pottery handle.

Note: Packing in the way suggested makes cutting into pats difficult, so it might be a good idea for the user to remove the butter from the containers and cut it into slices or cubes — as preferred. You could add this suggestion on a gift card.

Chive Butter *(for poultry, fish and meat grills)*

4oz (125g) unsalted butter, soft but not runny
6 rounded tsp very finely chopped fresh chives
white pepper to taste

1 Beat butter to a smooth cream then add chives and pepper to taste.
2 Continue to beat until very well mixed. Pack into containers straight away.

Packing   As Anchovy Butter.

Herb Butter *(for meat and fish grills)*

4oz (125g) unsalted butter, soft but not runny
1 level tbsp very finely chopped watercress leaves
1 level tbsp chopped parsley
1 level tbsp very finely chopped or grated onion
1 tsp lemon juice

1 Beat butter to a smooth cream, then add rest of ingredients.
2 Continue to beat until very well mixed. Pack into containers straight away.

Packing   As Anchovy Butter.

Mustard Butter *(for all meat and fish grills)*

4oz (125g) unsalted butter, soft but not runny
1-2 level tbsp prepared continental mustard (mild),
or 3 level tsp prepared English mustard
1 tsp lemon juice

1 Beat butter to a smooth cream, then add mustard and lemon juice.
2 Continue to beat until very well mixed. Pack into containers straight away.

Packing   As Anchovy Butter.

Lemon Butter *(for grilled and baked fish)*

4oz (125g) unsalted butter, soft but not runny
1 level tsp finely grated lemon peel
2 tsp lemon juice
white pepper to taste

1 Beat butter to smooth cream, then add the lemon.
2 Continue to beat until very well mixed. Season with pepper. Pack into containers straight away.

Packing   As Anchovy Butter.

Curry Butter *(for chicken and lamb grills)*

4oz (125g) unsalted butter, soft but not runny
3 rounded tsp curry powder
½ level tsp garam masala
1 tsp lemon juice

1 Beat butter to a smooth cream then add curry powder, garam masala and lemon juice.
2 Continue to beat until very well mixed. Pack into containers straight away.

Packing   As Anchovy Butter.

Garlic Butter *(for grilled steak, lamb and pork)*

4oz (125g) unsalted butter, soft but not runny
white pepper to taste
1 garlic clove, peeled and crushed

1 Beat butter to a smooth cream, then add garlic.
2 Continue to beat until very well mixed. Season with pepper. Pack into containers straight away.

Packing   As Anchovy Butter.

Sweet Hard Sauces

Essential, some people say for Christmas puddings, these Hard Sauces or Butters keep very well, provided they are stored in the refrigerator, and make lovely gifts.

Brandy Butter (Brandy Hard Sauce)

4oz (125g) butter, soft but not runny
3oz (75g) icing sugar, sifted
1oz (25g) caster sugar
2 tbsp brandy

1 Beat butter until very smooth. Add sugars and brandy.
2 Beat until mixture looks very light and creamy and is at least double its original volume. Pack straight away.

Packing   Spoon into wine-type glasses or small tumblers. Cover with cling film, then wrap tops in Christmas gift paper. Tie round with ribbon. Add a label to each.

Rum Butter (Rum Hard Sauce)

Make and pack exactly as Brandy Butter (Brandy Hard Sauce) but substitute dark rum for brandy.

Cumberland Rum Butter

Perfection on top of hot mince pies.

4oz (125g) butter, soft but not runny
4oz (125g) light brown soft sugar
1 level tsp mixed spice
2 tbsp dark rum

1 Beat butter until very smooth. Add sugar and spice and continue to beat until mixture is very light and fluffy.
2 Gradually whisk in rum, then pack into containers straight away.

Packing   As Brandy Butter.

5
Preserves – Jams and Chutneys

Preserves, meaning jams, marmalades and chutneys, make lovely, economical gifts for all age groups, adding charm and colour to kitchen and larder shelves. Here is a selection of old and new recipes.

Hints on Preserving

1 Choose fruit that is undamaged and only just ripe. Over-ripe fruit sometimes leads to failure and the preserve turning mouldy.

2 If using frozen fruit, add an extra 1oz (25g) fruit to every 8oz (225g) of it in the recipe to ensure a firm set.

3 Use a large, heavy-based pan. It should be only half-full *after* sugar has been added. To avoid the preserve boiling over, or having to be cooked for a very long time, it is better to make several small quantities rather than one big batch.

4 Always stir with a long-handled wooden spoon as it never gets hot. Metal does and can not only scratch the pan but also burn your hand.

5 Make sure fruit and/or vegetables are well cooked-down before the sugar is added.

6 After adding sugar, stir preserve over low heat until sugar dissolves, then boil briskly until setting point is reached (this only applies to jam and marmalade, *not* chutney).

7 It is wasteful to keep removing scum, as some of the preserve will be removed each time. Do so at the very end. Sometimes a knob of butter, stirred into the preserve when it has finished cooking, helps to disperse some of the scum.

8 To test if jam or marmalade has reached setting point, pour 1 tsp onto a cold saucer. Leave to stand 1 minute. If a skin forms on top which wrinkles when touched, then the jam, etc, is ready. For those with preserving thermometers, the temperature should register 150°C (220°F).

9 Leave preserve to cool off at least 10 minutes before carefully spooning into clean, dry and warm jars. Leave strawberry jam and marmalades in the pan until a skin forms on top, then stir round gently before potting: this way the fruit or peel will stay evenly distributed and will not rise to the tops of the jars.

10 Make sure jars are filled to the brim, as preserves have a tendency to shrink.

11 After filling, cover preserve in each pot with a well-fitting wax-paper disc. Wipe rims of jars clean, then cover with cellophane rounds, either while the preserve is very hot or after it is completely cold. Secure with elastic bands or string.

12 Label clearly (remembering to date) and store in a dark, dry and well-ventilated cupboard. The colours of preserves will fade if stored in a sunlit spot.

13 Some fruits, etc, lack natural pectin (the gel-like substance which works with acid in the fruit and makes the jam set), so where necessary I have added commercial liquid pectin, called Certo. This also gives you the opportunity of making more adventurous preserves, such as black cherry preserve and jelly marmalade.

Packing jams Label jars with ornamental or coloured labels, then cover tops (over the cellophane) with hand-crocheted rounds (close pattern and not too lacy), or with fabric cut round the edges with pinking shears. Tie round with fine cord, ribbon or coloured string. If liked, transport in a small basket lined with tissue paper.

Apple and Blackberry Jam *(makes 5lb or 2.5kg)*

1lb (450g) peeled cooking apples, cored and sliced
2lb (900g) blackberries, washed
¼pt (150ml) water
3lb (1.5kg) granulated or preserving sugar
½oz (15g) butter

1 Put fruit into pan with water. Bring to boil and lower heat. Cover. Simmer for 15-20 minutes or until fruit is soft and pulpy, crushing it with a fork every so often to break down the blackberries.
2 Add sugar and stir over low heat until dissolved. Increase heat and boil briskly until setting point is reached (see Hint no 8). Stir in butter to disperse scum.
3 Cool for about 10 minutes, then transfer to glass or pottery jars, filling to the brim. Top with wax-paper discs and cellophane covers.

Gooseberry Jam *(makes 5lb or 2.5kg)*

Follow recipe and method for Apple and Blackberry Jam, but use ¾pt (425ml) water and simmer fruit for a minimum of 30 minutes before adding sugar.

Gooseberry and Rhubarb Jam *(makes 5lb or 2.5kg)*

Follow recipe and method for Apple and Blackberry Jam, but use half gooseberries and half cut-up rhubarb. Simmer for 30 minutes in ½pt (275ml) water before adding sugar.

Blackcurrant Jam *(makes 5lb or 2.5kg)*

Follow recipe and method for Apple and Blackberry Jam, but use only 2½lb (just over 1 kg) stemmed blackcurrants, and increase water to 1½pt (840ml). Simmer very slowly for about 45-50 minutes or until skins are really tender.

Damson Jam *(makes 5lb or 2.5kg)*

Follow recipe and method for Apple and Blackberry Jam but use only 2½lb (just over 1kg) slit damsons and ¾pt (425ml) water. Simmer slowly for a minimum of 30 minutes before adding sugar. Remove stones from top at the very end.

Plum or Greengage Jam *(makes 5lb or 2.5kg)*

Follow recipe and method for Apple and Blackberry Jam, but increase water to ½pt (275ml) and simmer for 30 minutes before adding sugar. Remove stones at the end.

Raspberry or Loganberry Jam *(makes 5lb or 2.5kg)*

Follow recipe and method for Apple and Blackberry Jam but use 3lb (1.5kg) fruit, 3lb (1.5kg) sugar and *no water*. Crush berries over low heat in saucepan, simmer for 5 minutes, then add sugar. Dissolve slowly over low heat then continue as other jams, using Apple and Blackberry Jam as a guide.

Raspberry and Redcurrant Jam *(makes 5lb or 2.5kg)*

Follow recipe and method for Apple and Blackberry Jam, but use half raspberries, half stemmed redcurrants. Add ¼pt (150ml) water and simmer very slowly for a minimum of 30 minutes before adding sugar.

Black Cherry Jam *(makes about 5lb or 2.5kg)*

2½lb (just over 1kg) black cherries, in tip-top condition
6 tbsp lemon juice
¼pt (150ml) water
3lb (1.5kg) granulating or preserving sugar
1 bottle Certo

1 Halve cherries and stone. Put into large pan with lemon juice and water. Bring to boil. Lower heat. Cover.
2 Simmer gently for 15 minutes. Add sugar. Simmer, stirring, over low heat until sugar dissolves.

3 Increase heat and bring quickly to a rapid boil. Boil for 4 minutes. Remove from heat.

4 Stir in Certo and re-boil for a further minute. Remove from heat again, stir round and leave at least 15 minutes — or until a skin forms on top — before potting.

Lemon Shred Jelly (makes about 3 ½lb or 1.5kg)

1 heaped tbsp finely shredded lemon peel
1pt (575ml) water
¼ level tsp bicarbonate of soda (which helps to soften peel)
6fl oz (175ml) fresh lemon juice
2lb 10oz (1.175kg) granulated or preserving sugar
1 bottle of Certo

1 Put peel and water into pan with bicarbonate of soda. Bring to boil. Lower heat. Cover. Simmer for about 15 minutes or until peel is very soft.

2 Add lemon juice and sugar. Stir over low heat until sugar dissolves.

3 Bring to a rapid boil and boil for 1 minute. Remove from heat. Stir in Certo and re-boil for ½ minute.

4 Leave until lukewarm before potting and covering as other jams, using Apple and Blackberry Jam as a guide.

Marmalade (makes about 5lb or 2.5kg)

As marmalades can be tricky to make, and as there are any number of recipes and variations, I have picked out just two which I know work well and always please people. Their gleam is not as bright as marmalades made for competitions but that is what makes them, I believe, such an endearing gift. No beauty prizes here, no pretensions of grandeur either: but, the marmalades both taste delicious and look friendly and cheerful on the breakfast table.

1½lb (675g) bitter oranges (Seville)
3pt (1.75 litres) water
3 tbsp fresh lemon juice
3lb (1.5kg) sugar
½oz (15g) butter or margarine

1 Wash and dry oranges and put, as they are, into a large pan.

2 Add water and bring to boil. Lower heat. Cover. Simmer gently for 2 hours or until skins are very soft and can be easily punctured with a fork or skewer.

3 Take oranges out of pan with a draining spoon, and put onto an enamel plate. Cool slightly. Then, using a knife and fork, chop them up coarsely.
4 Keep all the pips, tie them in a small piece of material or transfer them to 2 coffee filter-bags, one inside the other for safety. Close securely.
5 Return chopped oranges, bag of pips and lemon juice to pan. Add sugar. Dissolve slowly over low heat, stirring.
6 Bring to boil and boil briskly until setting point is reached (see Hint no 8). Stir in butter to disperse scum.
7 Leave until marmalade is lukewarm and a skin forms on top. Stir round before potting and covering as jam (see Hint no 11).

Packing Pot in small, attractive jars, and cover in bright-orange, yellow or green fabric.

Mixed Fruit Marmalade *(makes 5lb or 2.5kg)*

Make as basic Marmalade above, but use 1½lb (675g) mixed citrus fruits such as grapefruit and sweet oranges. Whatever the combination, however, *do not* exclude lemon juice.

Apple Chutney *(makes about 5-6lb or 2.5-3kg)*

Adaptable and flavourful, chutneys are a typically British condiment. Many years ago, when we lived in a house with an orchard, I remember making enough chutney every autumn to keep friends, family and neighbours supplied all the year through! Always good with meat, eggs and cheeses, this is a standard apple chutney; and I give a few variations afterwards.

4lb (2kg) cooking apples
1lb (450g) onions
2 garlic cloves (optional)
water
8oz (225g) stoned dates in a block
4oz (125g) raisins
4oz (125g) sultanas
2pt (1.25 litres) malt vinegar
1½lb (675g) dark brown soft sugar

2 level tsp salt
2 bouquet-garni bags, tied together
2 level tsp ground ginger
3 level tsp cinnamon
1 level tsp allspice
2 bay leaves
¼ level tsp white pepper (or more if you like a hot chutney)

1 Peel and core apples. Peel and coarsely chop onions. Peel garlic if used. Mince all three together. Put into large, heavy pan with just enough water to cover.
2 Bring to boil, stirring. Lower heat. Add lid. Simmer slowly for about 15 minutes or until vegetables are tender. Uncover. Continue to cook until water evaporates completely.
3 Coarsely mince dates, raisins and sultanas. Add to pan with rest of ingredients.
4 Stir over low heat until sugar dissolves completely. Continue to cook, stirring occasionally, until chutney thickens to the consistency of jam. Do not cover.
5 Keep heat low to prevent chutney from burning, stir frequently; allow 1½-2 hours cooking time.
6 Remove bouquet-garni bags and bay leaves, then pot and cover as jam.

Packing Cover cellophane tops with rounds of gingham, then tie on with string.

Pear and Apple Chutney *(makes 5lb or 2.5kg)*

Make and pack as Apple Chutney, but use half pears and half apples.

Plum and Apricot Chutney *(makes 5lb or 2.5kg)*

Make and pack as Apple Chutney, but use half plums and half fresh apricots. If possible, remove stones before adding to pan. If not, remove them at the very end.

Green Tomato Chutney *(makes 5lb or 2.5kg)*

Make and pack as Apple Chutney, but use 5lb (2.5kg) cut-up green tomatoes instead of the 4lb apples.

6
Cakes

Bird of Paradise Cake

A heavenly cake laden with flaked almonds, juicy carrots and bananas. It stores well and is fairly easy to make.

2 large carrots
2 large, ripe bananas
8oz (225g) plain flour
1 level tsp baking powder
1 level tsp bicarbonate of soda
1 level tsp mixed spice or ground allspice
2oz (50g) butter or margarine
6oz (175g) soft brown sugar (light variety)
2 eggs (size 3), beaten (kitchen temperature)
1 tsp vanilla essence
¼ tsp almond essence
3oz (75g) flaked almonds, lightly toasted

1 Well-grease and paper-line a 7in (17.5cm) round cake tin. Preheat oven to 190°C (375°F), Gas 5.
2 Peel and wash carrots then finely grate. Mash bananas in a basin. Sift together flour, baking powder, bicarbonate of soda and spice.
3 Cream butter or margarine and sugar together till light and fluffy. Beat in eggs, essences and bananas. Gradually mix in dry ingredients with carrots and nuts. Stir till evenly combined.
4 Transfer to prepared tin and bake for about 50 minutes, when cake should be well-risen and golden-brown.

5 Remove from oven and cool for 15 minutes. Turn out on to a wire rack and peel away lining paper. Leave cake until completely cold before storing in an airtight tin (up to 3 days) in readiness for packing.

Packing If you feel like making someone a present of a cake tin as well as the cake, pop the cake back into the tin in which it was baked. Cover with cling film and wrap in fancy paper. Tie like a parcel, using ribbon. Alternatively, wrap the cake in cling film and top with a bow of ribbon.

The cake is very good iced, so you could box the cake with a packet of icing sugar and instructions for making simple glacé icing with lemon juice. Place the cake and sugar side by side and wrap with cling film. Tie with ribbon, finishing with a large bow.

Prune and Walnut Cake

Succulent and beautifully flavoured, this cake is a good keeper and would be ideal for a Christmas or Advent present.

12oz (350g) plain flour	1 rounded tsp finely grated orange peel
3 level tsp baking powder	
4oz (125g) soft brown sugar (light variety)	4oz (125g) stoned prunes, finely chopped
½pt (275ml) cold milk	3oz (75g) walnuts, finely chopped
1 egg (size 3), beaten	
3oz (75g) butter or margarine, melted	

1 Well-grease and paper-line a 7in (17.5cm) round cake tin. Preheat oven to 190°C (375°F), Gas 5.
2 Sift flour and baking powder into a bowl. Toss in sugar. Pour in milk, well-mixed with egg and butter or margarine, then add orange peel, prunes and walnuts.
3 Mix all ingredients well together, stirring briskly without beating. Transfer to prepared tin.
4 Bake for 40-45 minutes or until cake is well-risen and golden-brown.
5 Remove from oven and cool for 15 minutes. Turn out on to a wire rack and peel away lining paper. Leave cake until completely cold before storing in an airtight tin (up to 3 days) in readiness for packing.

Packing Follow directions for Bird of Paradise Cake.

No-bake Garland Cake

A pretty affair, well-suited for Christmas and Easter, and a cake which 'cooks' in the refrigerator, not in the oven.

- 4oz (125g) butter (not margarine for this one)
- 6oz (175g) marshmallows, cut into small pieces with wetted scissors
- 1lb (450g) chocolate digestive biscuits, crushed
- 2 level tsp mixed spice
- 8oz (225g) mixed dried fruit
- 1 level tsp finely grated orange peel
- 2oz (50g) glacé cherries, coarsely chopped
- 2oz (50g) stoned dates, coarsely chopped
- 2oz (50g) brazil nuts, thinly sliced
- juice of 2 large lemons

1 Line a 2lb (1kg) loaf tin with Bakewell non-stick parchment paper.
2 Melt butter on a low heat in a saucepan with 2oz (50g) of the cut-up marshmallows.
3 Tip biscuits into a large bowl, then toss in spice, dried fruit, orange peel, cherries, dates and nuts.
4 Pour melted butter and marshmallows over crumb mixture, then add lemon juice and remaining marshmallows.
5 Mix all ingredients well together with finger-tips and press into prepared tin. Cover. Refrigerate overnight.
6 Take out of tin, remove lining paper and wrap cake in foil. Store in the refrigerator. Cut into medium-thick slices for serving.

Packing Leave in foil or wrap in cellophane. Tie round with ribbon, finishing with a bow.

Dutch Chocolate Refrigerator Cake

Another 'no-bake' cake which is luxuriously rich, sophisticated and perfect for a very special occasion, such as an anniversary or adult birthday party.

- 1 egg (size 3)
- 1oz (25g) caster sugar
- 8oz (225g) plain chocolate, melted in basin over pan of hot water
- 8oz (225g) Dutch unsalted butter, melted
- half of the finely grated peel and juice of a medium-sized orange
- 3 tbsp Grand Marnier or Tia Maria
- 2oz (50g) glacé cherries, chopped
- 3oz (75g) hazel nuts, unskinned and coarsely chopped
- 8oz (225g) plain digestive biscuits, broken into small pieces

1 Whisk egg and sugar together until the consistency of whipped cream; mixture should balloon up to just over ¼pt (150ml).
2 Add chocolate and butter. Mix thoroughly. Stir in all remaining ingredients, then transfer to a 7in (17.5cm) loose-based round cake tin, lined with Bakewell non-stick parchment paper.
3 Refrigerate overnight. Remove from tin and peel away lining paper. Carefully transfer to a silver cakeboard covered with a doily. Store in the refrigerator until ready for packing.

Packing Leave cake on doily-covered board and transfer to a large box. Pad round with crumpled tissue paper, then wrap in cling film. Decorate with a spray of artificial or fresh flowers. If, for example, the cake is to be given to a couple celebrating their silver wedding, a silver-plated cake server would be an appropriate addition.

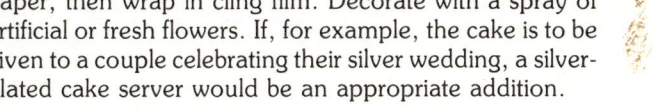

My Favourite Christmas Cake

A tried and trusted cake which has served me well over the years and which I have made over and over again to give away to friends and family, and also to enjoy at home over the festive season. It can just as easily serve for birthdays and anniversaries, as it keeps well and can be covered with almond paste and royal icing. Alternatively, it can have its top studded with 2oz (50g) blanched and split almonds and be treated as a Dundee cake.

7oz (200g) plain flour
1oz (25g) cocoa powder
1 level tsp cinnamon
1 level tsp ground ginger
1 level tsp ground allspice
8oz (225g) butter, softened
8oz (225g) soft brown sugar (dark variety)
1 level tbsp black treacle
2 level tsp finely grated orange peel
1 level tsp finely grated lemon peel
4 eggs (size 3)
2¼lb (just over 1kg) mixed dried fruit including peel
2oz (50g) walnuts or hazelnuts, finely chopped
2oz (50g) stoned dates, chopped
2oz (50g) glacé cherries, chopped
1 tbsp sherry

1 Well grease an 8in (20cm) round cake tin, then line base and sides with greased greaseproof paper. Pre-heat oven to 150°C (300°F), Gas 2.

2 Sift first five ingredients on to a large plate. In large bowl, cream butter, sugar, treacle and both orange and lemon peels together until light and fluffy.

3 Break eggs, one at a time, into a cup to check for freshness. Tip into creamed mixture individually each with 1 tbsp of dried ingredients. Beat in thoroughly.

4 Stir in mixed dried fruit, nuts, dates, cherries and sherry. Finally fold in rest of dry ingredients with a large metal spoon or plastic spatula.

5 Spread smoothly into prepared tin and bake in oven centre for about 3-3¼ hours or until very thin skewer, pushed gently into middle of cake, comes out clean, with no uncooked mixture clinging to it.

6 When ready, the cake should be well-risen and golden, but if it seems to be browning too much, cover top with a circle of brown paper.

7 Remove from oven and leave to stand for 30 minutes in tin. Carefully turn out on to a wire rack and leave until completely cold.

8 Remove lining paper, then store cake in an airtight tin until ready for packing.

Packing Tie a cake frill round sides of cake, then wrap in cling film. Pack in a box with 1lb (450g) prepared almond paste (bought keeps better than home-made) and a packet (just over 1lb or 500g) of icing sugar. Include also some Christmas ornaments. The recipient can then decorate the cake according to personal taste.

For a Dundee cake, use tartan fabric or paper and attach a miniature bottle of whisky and a sprig of heather.

Mincemeat Cake

An unusual cake, based on fruit mincemeat (the kind used for mince pies), crushed cornflakes and sweetened condensed milk. It contains no additional fat but has a moist and succulent flavour and should be allowed to mature for at least 1 week in an airtight tin.

1lb (450g) mincemeat
1lb 2oz (500g) mixed dried fruit including peel
4oz (125g) walnuts, coarsely chopped
8oz (225g) cornflakes, crushed fairly finely
3 eggs (size 3), well-beaten
1 large can sweetened condensed milk
½ level tsp cinnamon
1 level tsp mixed spice
¼ level tsp ground nutmeg
¼ level tsp ground ginger

1 Prepare an 8in (20cm) tin exactly as for My Favourite Christmas Cake (previous recipe). Preheat oven to 150°C (300°F), Gas 2.

2 Put all cake ingredients into a large bowl and, using a large wooden spoon, work together until thoroughly mixed.

3 Spread evenly into prepared tin and bake for 2 hours in centre of oven. When ready, the cake should be a deep golden colour and feel firm to the touch.

4 Remove from oven and leave to stand for 30 minutes. Turn out on to a wire rack; remove lining paper when cake is completely cold. Store in an airtight tin for 1 week before packing.

Packing Follow suggestions for My Favourite Christmas Cake.

Choc Nut Cake

A delicious cake that suits any occasion, from a bridge party to an evening gathering of friends. Make it, bake it, pack it and take it, and you can't go far wrong!

1 bar (3½oz or 100g) plain chocolate, refrigerated
9oz (250g) butter or block margarine, softened
7oz (200g) caster sugar
4 eggs (size 3), at room temperature, well-beaten
10oz (275g) self-raising flour
½oz (15g) cornflour
5oz (125-50g) walnuts, coarsely chopped

1 Brush a 10in (25cm) spring-clip cake tin (the kind used for cheese-cake, with loose base and hinged sides) with melted butter. Line base with greased greaseproof paper. Preheat oven to 190°C (375°F), Gas 5.

2 Chop chocolate into small pieces or grate finely. Alternatively, grind coarsely in food processor or blender.
3 Cream butter or margarine and sugar together until light and fluffy. Gradually beat in eggs, adding a tablespoon or two of flour and cornflour sifted together towards the end to prevent mixture from curdling.
4 Stir in chocolate and nuts. Lastly fold in sifted dry ingredients with a large metal spoon. Spread smoothly into prepared tin and bake for 1¼ hours when cake should be well-risen and brown.
5 Remove from oven and leave to stand for 15 minutes. Unclip sides, then invert cake on to a wire rack. Remove base and lining paper. Leave until completely cold, then store in an airtight tin until ready to pack.

Packing Wrap cake completely in cling film, then pack in a box lined with doilies. Wrap in cellophane paper, then tie on a greetings card. Alternatively, cover with cling film and wrap in a novelty tea-towel.

Gingerbread

A good keeper which is ideal for Hallowe'en.

4oz (125g) lard or white cooking fat	2 eggs (size 3)
2oz (50g) light brown soft sugar	8oz (225g) plain flour
	1 level tsp mixed spice
4oz (125g) golden syrup	3 level tsp ground ginger
4oz (125g) black treacle	½ level tsp cinnamon
¼pt (150ml) cold milk	1 level tsp bicarbonate of soda

1 Line a greased roasting tin, measuring about 10 × 8in (25 × 20cm), with greaseproof paper or Bakewell non-stick parchment paper. If using greaseproof, brush with melted fat. Preheat oven to 160°C (325°F), Gas 3.
2 Place lard or cooking fat, sugar, syrup and treacle into a saucepan. Melt over very low heat. Beat milk and eggs well together.
3 Sift flour, spice, ginger, cinnamon and bicarbonate of soda into a bowl. Make a well in the centre. Pour in beaten milk and eggs followed by melted ingredients.
4 Using a fork, mix to a smooth batter, stirring briskly without beating. Transfer mixture to prepared tin and bake 1-1¼ hours or until gingerbread is well-risen and a wooden cocktail stick, pushed gently into centre, comes

out clean with no uncooked mixture clinging to it.
5 Remove from oven and leave to stand for 15 minutes. Turn out on to wire rack and leave until completely cold before removing lining paper. Store in an airtight tin until ready for packing.

Packing Wrap in aluminium foil. If for Hallowe'en, decorate with witches' hats, broomsticks and assorted cats cut from black paper. Secure to foil with glue. If for any other occasion, wrap in foil, then wrap in a checked tea-towel, or a square of gingham trimmed round the edges with pinking shears. Alternatively, stand foil-wrapped cake on a wooden board, add a cake knife and wrap with cellophane for a more costly present.

Mince Pies *(makes 12)*

I can think of no nicer way of saying 'Happy Xmas' than with homemade mince pies. Here is a tried and trusted recipe made with mock rough puff pastry.

8oz (225g) self-raising flour	½oz (15g) caster sugar
pinch of salt	3-4 tbsp cold milk
4½oz (140g) mixture butter or margarine with lard or cooking fat	12oz (350g) mincemeat beaten egg for brushing the tops

1 Sift flour and salt into bowl. Rub in fats finely. Toss in sugar. Using a knife, mix to a fairly stiff dough with the milk.
2 Wrap in foil and chill for 30 minutes. Turn out on to a floured surface and knead lightly until smooth. Roll out fairly thinly.
3 Cut into 12 rounds with a 3½in (9cm) biscuit cutter and 12 smaller rounds with a 2½in (6cm) cutter.
4 Use the larger rounds to line 12 deepish, lightly greased bun tins. Fill with equal amounts of mincemeat, then top with the smaller rounds of pastry to form lids. Press down lightly with finger tips.
5 Brush tops with beaten egg, then bake until golden-brown, allowing 20-25 minutes at 220°C (425°F), Gas 7.
6 Remove from oven, cool down for 10 minutes, then carefully transfer to a wire rack. Store the cooked pies in an airtight tin when completely cold and leave until ready for packing.

Packing Arrange on a pretty cake stand or plate, lined with silver or gold doilies. Dust with sifted icing sugar then cover completely with cling film. Add a Christmas gift tag. Alternatively, pack into a box or tin, decorated as described in Chapter 1, and instead of dusting pies with icing sugar, include a small pack in the box or tin.

Linz Cake

A speciality jam tart from Austria, this is one of my own particular favourites and makes a marvellous gift for those who appreciate cakes that are a little out-of-the-ordinary. The version below serves 12 generously.

8oz (225g) unsalted Dutch, Danish or French butter, softened
8oz (225g) caster sugar
8oz (225g) plain flour
2 level tsp cinnamon
4oz (125g) shelled but unskinned hazelnuts, finely ground*
4oz (125g) shelled but unskinned almonds finely ground*
1 egg (size 3), separated
rapberry jam
beaten egg
icing sugar

1 Cream butter and sugar well together, then knead in flour and cinnamon (sifted together), nuts and egg yolk. Use either finger-tips or a fork.
2 Form into a smooth ball, wrap in foil and refrigerate for 1 hour until firm.
3 Press three-quarters of the pastry to form an 8in (20cm) round on a lightly greased baking tray. Use a plate as a cutting guide and pinch up edges between finger and thumb to form a low 'wall'.
4 Fill with raspberry jam, then cover with a criss-cross of pastry, rolled and cut from the reserved quarter of pastry. Press edges of strips well onto the edge of tart so that they hold in place.
5 Brush tart (not jam) with lightly beaten egg white and bake for 50-60 minutes in oven set to 150°C (300°F), Gas 3. When ready, the tart should be a warm golden colour; allow a little longer if it remains on the pale side.
6 Remove from oven and leave to stand for 10 minutes. Transfer to wire rack and leave until completely cold. Store in an airtight container until ready for packing.
*Use a blender, coffee grinder or food processor for grinding nuts.

Packing Line an attractive box with lacy doilies and stand the Linz Cake on top. Stand a little packet of icing sugar beside it for dusting over top. Wrap in cling film. Parcel up in floral paper, ribbon and a bow.

Meringue Basket

This makes an enchanting gift, especially in summer when it can be filled with strawberries or raspberries and cream. One of the best things about meringues is that they store perfectly in any airtight container and keep more-or-less indefinitely. Thus you can prepare a basket well ahead of time.

2 whites from size 2 eggs	5oz (150g) caster sugar
pinch of cream of tartar or a squeeze of lemon	3 level tsp cornflour

1 Brush a shallow baking tray with oil. Line with Bakewell non-stick parchment paper, greaseproof paper or foil. *Do not brush any of these with grease or oil at all* or the meringue basket will stick.
2 Beat whites to a stiff snow with cream of tartar or lemon juice. Gradually beat in two-thirds of the sugar, and continue beating until meringue is very shiny and stands in tall, non-collapsible peaks when the beaters are lifted out.
3 Fold in rest of sugar with cornflour. Using a plate as a guide, outline an 8in (20cm) circle on the paper. Fill in with meringue, then build up sides to form a raised edge of about 1in (2½cm) all the way round. Do this with the back of a teaspoon.
4 Place in oven preheated to 110°C (225°F), Gas ¼. Bake for 3½ hours or until basket is pale cream, crisp and biscuity.
5 Remove from oven and leave to stand for 10 minutes. Carefully lift away from paper and turn upside-down. Return to tray (still lined).
6 Continue to dry out in the oven for a further 30-45 minutes, then cool on a wire rack. Store in an airtight tin when completely cold or in a large box which must be filled with tissue paper and then well sealed.

Packing A meringue basket is so pretty that it justifies decorative packing. Therefore choose a large box or tin and decorate as described in Chapter 1. Surround the basket with crumpled tissue paper to avoid breakage, then cover with cling film or lid. Decorate with a bow of satin ribbon and a large cream-silk artificial flower. Present with a box of soft fruit and a carton of cream.

American-style Chocolate Brownies *(makes about 20 pieces)*

Dark and fudge-like in consistency, these are an 'anytime' gift and particularly popular with boys of all ages.

3oz (75g) plain flour
1½oz (40g) cocoa powder
½ level tsp baking powder
4oz (125g) butter or margarine, softened
8oz (225g) light brown soft sugar
1 tsp vanilla essence
2 eggs (size 2), at room temperature

1 Sift together the first three ingredients. Cream butter or margarine and sugar together until light and fluffy. Beat in essence and eggs.
2 Using a large metal spoon or spatula, fold in dry ingredients and transfer to an 11 × 7in (27.5 × 17.5cm) Swiss-roll tin, greased and lined with greaseproof paper.
3 Spread smoothly with a knife, then bake until risen and brown – about 25-30 minutes in oven set to 180°C (350°F), Gas 4.
4 Remove from oven, cool to lukewarm, then cut into about 20 pieces. Cool on a wire rack and store in an airtight tin until ready for packing.

Packing Pack in a shallow box (see Chapter 1), lined with foil, and wrap with more foil. Decorate with blue and red stars-and-stripes, cut from coloured gummed paper.

Fruited Bran Loaf

With all the interest in health foods, this loaf should please those who like a non-rich fruit cake. It is delicious served sliced with butter.

4oz (125g) All-Bran
5oz (150g) light brown soft sugar
4oz (125g) stoned cooking dates, finely chopped
4oz (125g) mixed dried fruit, including peel
2oz (50g) unsalted peanuts or walnuts
½pt (275ml) cold milk
4oz (125g) self-raising flour, sifted

1 Place All-Bran, sugar, dates, dried fruit and nuts into a bowl. Stir in milk and leave to soak for 30 minutes.
2 Gently stir in flour with large metal spoon. Transfer mixture to greased and paper-lined 2lb (1kg) loaf tin. Bake for 1 hour in oven set to 180°C (350°F), Gas 4.
3 Remove from oven and leave to stand for 10 minutes. Turn out on to wire rack and peel away lining paper when cold. Store in an airtight tin until needed.

Packing Wrap in cling film, then wrap in sacking (or coarse hessian), tying ends with string to make the package look like a large cracker. The whole effect should be rustic and wholesome. If liked, pack in a box at the last minute with a packet of unsalted butter and an attractive cake knife. If you are superstitious, ask the recipient to give you a penny for the knife, to prevent a break in the friendship!

Malt Loaf

A teatime special to take with you if you have been invited out to tea — but make at least three days ahead as the loaf needs time to mature.

8oz (225g) wholemeal flour
2 level tsp baking powder
1oz (25g) butter or margarine
2oz (50g) caster sugar
2oz (50g) raisins
1oz (25g) currants
1 level tbsp malt extract
1 level tbsp golden syrup
1 level tbsp black treacle
¼pt (125ml) cold milk

1 Mix flour and baking powder in mixing bowl. Rub in fat finely then toss in sugar, raisins and currants.
2 Place malt extract, syrup and treacle into a sturdy pan and melt over a low heat.
3 Pour over dry ingredients, add milk, then fork-mix all ingredients well together.
4 Transfer to a greased and paper-lined 1lb (500g) loaf tin and bake until firm; about 45-50 minutes in oven set to 190°C (375°F), Gas 5.
5 Remove from oven and cool for 10 minutes. Turn out on to wire rack and peel away lining paper when cold. Store in an airtight tin till ready for packing.

Packing Stand on an attractive plate lined with doilies and wrap in cling film. For a festive look, wrap again in brightly coloured cellophane paper, gathering up ends over top of loaf and tying with ribbon.

7
Puddings

The only puddings suitable for giving away are the ones that keep, and this brings us automatically to Christmas puddings. Below are a selection, all of which have something different about them to please everybody.

Yeasted Christmas Pudding *(makes four 1pt (575ml) puddings; each serves about 8)*

A stunning pudding, somewhat lightened by the original use of yeast, with a fragrant flavour and moist texture.

- 1lb (450g) mixed dried fruit, including peel
- 4oz (125g) stoned dates, chopped
- 8oz (125g) dried apricots, scissor-snipped into small pieces
- 2oz (50g) glacé cherries, chopped
- 2oz (50g) stoned prunes, chopped
- finely grated peel and juice of 1 large washed-and-dried orange
- 2 level tsp ground allspice
- 1 level tsp ground cinnamon
- ½pt (275ml) Guinness
- 12oz (350g) fresh white breadcrumbs
- 6oz (175g) plain flour, sifted
- 8oz (225g) dark brown soft sugar
- 8oz (225g) shredded suet
- 3 level tbsp dried yeast
- 2 level tsp caster sugar
- ¼pt (150ml) warm milk
- 5 eggs (size 3), beaten

1 Tip all the dried fruits into a large bowl. Stir in grated orange peel and juice, spices and Guinness.

2 In separate bowl, mix together crumbs, flour, brown sugar and suet. Mix yeast with caster sugar and milk. Leave in warm place to stand for about 20 minutes or until foamy. Add to crumb mixture.

3 Work in fruits and eggs, using a large wooden spoon or fork. If mixture seems very stiff, add two or three tablespoons more warm milk.

4 Divide between four 1pt (575ml) well-greased basins. Cover securely with greased greaseproof paper, then with foil. Secure by tying with string.

5 Steam each pudding steadily for 5 hours. Cool in basins. Cover with foil or cling-film and store in a cool pantry or larder (or refrigerator if space permits) until ready for packing. Tell the recipient, on a label, to re-steam each pudding for 2 hours before serving.

Packing See page 49.

Traditional 'Plum' Pudding *(makes two 2½pt (1.5 litre) puddings; each serves about 12)*

- 4oz (125g) plain flour
- ½oz (15g) cocoa powder
- 2 level tsp instant coffee powder
- 2 level tsp mixed spice
- 8oz (225g) fresh white breadcrumbs
- 10oz (275g) shredded suet
- 8oz (225g) dark brown soft sugar
- 1½lb (675g) mixed dried fruit to include currants, raisins and sultanas
- 2oz (50g) mixed chopped peel
- 2oz (50g) glacé cherries, chopped
- 4oz (125g) walnuts or brazils, coarsely chopped (or use mixture of nuts)
- finely grated peel of one medium washed-and-dried lemon
- finely grated peel of one medium washed-and-dried clementine or tangerine
- ½ tsp almond essence
- ½ tsp vanilla essence
- 4 eggs (size 2), beaten
- 2 tbsp whisky or dry sherry
- 1 level tbsp black treacle
- ¼pt (150ml) brown ale or dry cider

1 Sift flour, cocoa, coffee and spice into bowl. Toss in crumbs, suet, sugar, dried fruit, peel, cherries, nuts, and lemon and clementine or tangerine peel.

2 Stir in all remaining ingredients. Mix thoroughly. Cover with cloth. Leave to stand overnight in a cool place.

3 Divide equally between prepared basins. Cover as Yeasted Christmas Pudding. Steam each one steadily for 6 hours. Cool in basin.

4 Cover with foil or cling film and store in a cool pantry or larder or refrigerator (if space permits) until ready for packing.

5 Re-steam each pudding for 2½ hours before serving.

Packing See page 49.

Christmas Pudding Without Suet *(makes one pudding; serves about 12)*

For friends or family who adore Christmas pudding but have to watch their animal-fat intake, here is a version based on sunflower oil, skimmed milk and only one egg. It is surprisingly good, well-flavoured, and obviously lighter than the more traditional pudding.

4oz (125g) self-raising flour
1½ level tsp mixed spice
4oz (125g) fresh white breadcrumbs
4oz (125g) dark brown soft sugar
1lb (450g) mixed dried fruit including peel
2oz (50g) walnuts or toasted almond flakes, coarsely chopped
4 tbsp sunflower oil
5 tbsp skimmed milk
2 tbsp rum or whisky
1 level tbsp black treacle
1 egg (size 3), beaten

1 Sift flour and spice into bowl. Toss in crumbs, sugar, fruit and nuts.

2 Stir in oil, milk, rum or whisky, treacle and egg. Mix thoroughly, using a fork.

3 Transfer to a 2½pt (1.5 litre) well-greased pudding basin. Cover as Yeasted Christmas Pudding.

4 Steam for 5 hours. Cool in basin then cover with cling film or foil. Store in a cool, dry and airy place until ready for packing. Alternatively, store in the refrigerator.

5 Re-steam for 1½ hours before serving.

Packing See page 49.

Christmas Pudding Without Eggs *(makes one pudding; serves about 12)*

Over the years, I have had many requests for cakes and puddings without eggs, usually for dietetic or allergic reasons. This fruit-packed pudding works well and has an excellent, robust flavour.

4oz (125g) self-raising flour	1lb (450g) mixed dried fruit, including peel
1 level tsp mixed spice	
2 level tsp cinnamon	2oz (50g) walnuts, brazils, or unskinned hazelnuts, coarsely chopped
¼ level tsp ground ginger	
¼ level tsp nutmeg	
4oz (125g) fresh white breadcrumbs	¼pt (150ml) cider or Guinness
5oz (150g) shredded suet	3 tbsp sweet sherry
4oz (125g) dark brown soft sugar	3 tbsp cold milk
	2 tbsp orange squash
2oz (50g) ground almonds	

1 Sift flour, spice, cinnamon, ginger and nutmeg into bowl. Toss in crumbs, suet, sugar, almonds, fruit and nuts.
2 Add rest of ingredients and mix in well. Transfer to a 2½pt (1.5 litre) well-greased basin. Cover as Yeasted Christmas Pudding.
3 Steam steadily for 6 hours. Cool in basin. Cover with cling film or foil and store in a cool, dry and airy place until ready for packing. Re-steam for 2 hours before serving.

Packing Leave pudding in the basin, and stand in the middle of a square of checked or prettily patterned cotton material trimmed round the edges with pinking shears. Draw edges together over top of pudding and tie with ribbon. Transfer to decorated box and pack with Rum or Brandy Butter (see Chapter 4). Wrap completely in cellophane or, if box has a well-fitting lid, use that instead. Add a card with instructions for re-heating, flaming and serving. Alternatively, tie up in bright red or green cloth, add a sprig of holly and attach a miniature bottle of brandy, whisky or rum for flaming.

8
Biscuits

I offer a selection of biscuits to suit any and every occasion, from coffee morning to Christmas celebrations. Most biscuits keep several weeks if stored in airtight containers.

Shrewsbury Easter Biscuits

Old-fashioned biscuits flavoured with caraway seeds.

8oz (225g) plain flour	4oz (125g) caster sugar
½ level tsp mixed spice	2 level tsp caraway seeds
4oz (125g) butter or block margarine	1 egg (size 3), beaten
	a few tsp cold milk to mix

1 Sift flour and salt into bowl. Rub in butter or margarine finely. Toss in sugar and caraway seeds.
2 Add egg, then fork-mix to a stiff dough with milk. Foil-wrap and chill for ½ hour in the refrigerator. Divide equally into 24 pieces and place on two greased baking trays, leaving each biscuit room to expand.
3 Flatten with base of tumbler dipped in flour, then bake until pale gold, allowing 15-20 minutes in oven set to 180°C (350°F), Gas 4.
4 Cool on trays for 5 minutes, then transfer carefully to

wire racks. Cool completely. Store in an airtight tin until ready for packing.

Packing Pack carefully in a doily-lined box in layers, with tissue paper between. Cover with lid if it fits, or wrap with coloured cellophane paper. If liked, decorate with a couple of Easter chicks or some miniature chocolate Easter eggs.

Chocolate Crisps

Luscious little biscuits which need no rolling.

4oz (125g) butter or margarine, softened but not runny	½ tsp vanilla essence
	4oz (125g) plain flour
	1oz (25g) cocoa powder
2oz (25g) light brown soft sugar	icing sugar

1 Cream butter or margarine and sugar together until light and fluffy. Beat in essence.
2 Sift together flour and cocoa powder. Fork-stir into creamed ingredients.
3 Divide into 12 equal pieces and roll into balls. Stand on large well-greased baking tray, leaving each one room to spread.
4 Flatten slightly by pressing down with prongs of a fork, then bake 13-15 minutes in oven set to 190°C (375°F), Gas 5.
5 Cool on trays for 5 minutes, then transfer to wire rack. Leave until cold and dust with sifted icing sugar. Store in an airtight tin before packing.

Packing Arrange in single layer in decorated box (see Chapter 1), then cover securely with cling film.

Chocolate Melting Moments

Follow recipe and method for Chocolate Crisps, but after shaping the 12 pieces of mixture in balls, toss in porridge oats to cover. Place well apart on large greased baking tray and top each with half a glacé cherry. Bake as Chocolate Crisps.

Packing As Chocolate Crisps.

Dutch Choc Cherry Cookies

Dainty, crisp biscuits which are delicious after dinner with coffee, or served with afternoon tea.

3oz (75g) Dutch butter
6oz (175g) light brown soft sugar
½ tsp almond or vanilla essence
1 egg (size 3), beaten
6oz (175g) self-raising flour, sifted
2oz (50g) washed glacé cherries, dried and coarsely chopped
2oz (50g) chocolate dots or chopped plain chocolate

1 Cream butter, sugar and essence well together. Gradually beat in egg.
2 Using a fork, stir in flour, cherries and chocolate. Divide into 20 pieces and roll into balls between hands.
3 Transfer to two well-greased baking trays, leaving room for the biscuits to spread.
4 Bake until pale gold, allowing 12-15 minutes in oven set to 180°C (350°F), Gas 4.
5 Leave on trays for about 5 minutes, then transfer to wire racks. When completely cold, store in an airtight container.

Packing Transfer to any kind of glass jar with stopper or, if you can find one, a secondhand biscuit barrel with lid. Alternatively, pack into a box or tin, wrap with fancy paper and tie with ribbon.

Almond Shortbread

I made this up one day when I was desperately searching around for an original gift to take to someone who I knew appreciated homemade biscuits. I left the Shortbreads in the tin in which they were baked (sandwich tins are not *that* expensive to buy and make a re-useable and practical container) and the result was super.

4oz (125g) butter, softened but not runny
2oz (50g) caster sugar
6oz (175g) plain flour
1-1½oz (25-40g) flaked almonds

1 Cream butter and sugar together until light and fluffy, then work in flour, using a fork.
2 When well-combined, spread in 7in (17.5cm) lightly greased sandwich tin. Spread smoothly with a knife.
3 Tip almonds over top; then with flat of hand, press

well down into shortbread so it is completely covered.
4 Bake for 45 minutes in oven set to 160°C (325°F), Gas 3. Remove from oven and cool.
5 While slightly warm, cut into 8 or 12 triangles and carefully remove from tin. Transfer to wire rack.
6 Clean sandwich tin and return shortbread triangles when they are completely cold.

Packing Cover top with foil then wrap with fancy paper — tartan if you can find it. Tie round with ribbon.

Orange Flapjack

An easy crispy biscuit which is quick to make and delicious to eat.

5oz (150g) butter, softened but not runny	5oz (150g) golden syrup
1oz (25g) light brown soft sugar	1 level tsp finely grated orange peel
	8oz (225g) porridge oats

1 Put butter, sugar, syrup and rind into a saucepan. Stand over low heat until butter and sugar have melted.
2 Remove from heat. Stir in oats, then spread mixture evenly into well-greased large Yorkshire-pudding tin.
3 Bake until well-browned, allowing about 40 minutes in oven set to 180°C (350°F), Gas 4.
4 Remove from oven and cool for 10 minutes. Cut into about 16-18 pieces and transfer to wire rack until cold. Store in an airtight tin prior to packing.

Packing Pack into a doily-lined tin with well-fitting lid, a storage jar with stopper, or a basket. If using basket, wrap securely with cling film to keep the biscuits crisp.

Wheatmeal Biscuits

Semi-sweet biscuits which team well with cheese after a meal, or with coffee for elevenses.

3oz (75g) wholemeal flour	2oz (50g) light brown soft sugar
1oz (25g) oatmeal	
2oz (50g) butter or block margarine	about 3 tbsp cold milk to mix

1 Tip flour and oatmeal into bowl. Rub in butter or margarine finely.

2 Toss in sugar, then, using a fork for stirring, mix to a stiff dough with cold milk.

3 Turn out on to floured board, knead lightly until smooth, then roll out fairly thinly.

4 Cut into about 10-12 rounds with 2in (5cm) cutter, re-rolling and re-cutting trimmings to give the required quantity of biscuits.

5 Transfer to greased baking tray and bake until golden, allowing 15-20 minutes in oven set to 190°C (375°F), Gas 5.

6 Remove from oven, leave on trays for a few minutes, then transfer to a wire cooling rack.

7 Store in an airtight tin until ready for packing.

Packing Transfer to tin with well-fitting lid or carefully place in polythene bag, tie round and transfer to a swag-bag or sack (see Chapter 1).

Coffee Biscuits

Tempting biscuits for teatime which can, if liked, be sandwiched together with buttercream.

6oz (175g) plain flour	5oz (150g) butter or block margarine, softened but not runny
2oz (50g) semolina or rice flour	
2 level tsp instant coffee powder	4oz (125g) caster sugar
	1 egg yolk from size 3 egg
	cold milk

1 Sift together flour, semolina or rice flour and coffee powder.

2 Rub in butter or margarine finely then toss in sugar.

3 Using fork, mix to a stiff dough with egg yolk and 3-4 tsp cold milk.

4 Draw mixture together with finger-tips, wrap in foil and chill in the refrigerator for ½ hour.

5 Roll out thinly on floured surface and cut into 17-18 rounds with a 2in (5cm) biscuit cutter.

6 Transfer to two large greased trays and bake 15-18 minutes in oven set to 180°C (350°F), Gas 4.

7 Remove from oven and cool for 5 minutes. Transfer to wire cooling rack and store when completely cold in an airtight tin until ready to pack.

Packing As Orange Flapjacks.

Grantham Gingerbread Biscuits

Traditional biscuits which will be popular with those who like ginger.

4oz (125g) butter or block margarine, softened but not runny
4oz (125g) caster sugar
4oz (125g) plain flour
2 rounded tsp ground ginger
1 tbsp well-beaten egg

1 Cream butter or margarine and sugar together until light and fluffy.
2 Sift together flour and ginger. Using a fork, work into creamed ingredients with the beaten egg.
3 When well-mixed, divide equally into 15 pieces and roll each into a ball. Place on well-greased baking tray, leaving plenty of room between them for spreading.
4 Bake slowly allowing 45 minutes in oven set to 150°C (300°F), Gas 2.
5 Remove from oven, cool biscuits for about 5 minutes, then carefully transfer to wire rack.
6 Store when cold in an airtight container, prior to packing.

Packing   As Wheatmeal Biscuits.

Spicy Snaps

Winter biscuits, in my opinion, and just right for Hallowe'en.

6oz (175g) plain flour
1 level tsp allspice
½ level tsp cinnamon
3 level tsp ground ginger
3oz (75g) light brown soft sugar
3oz (75g) butter or margarine
2 level tbsp golden syrup
1 level tbsp black treacle
¼ level tsp bicarbonate of soda
1 tbsp cold milk
caster sugar for sprinkling

1 Sift flour and spices into bowl. Toss in sugar. Melt butter or margarine, syrup and treacle very gently in pan. Cool. Mix bicarbonate of soda with milk.
2 Add melted mixture to dry ingredients, together with soda and milk.
3 Fork-mix thoroughly, then shape into 24 balls. Transfer to two well-greased large baking trays, leaving room between each as they spread.
5 Press down lightly with prongs of a fork then sprinkle

with sugar. Bake for 23-25 minutes in oven set to 180°C (350°F), Gas 4. Remove from oven and leave to stand for 5 minutes.
6 Cool on a wire rack and store in an airtight tin.

Packing Pack in a large stoneware jar with cork 'lid', or in glass storage jar with well-fitting stopper. Wrap with brown paper and tie with bright ribbon. Alternatively, wrap in rustic-looking wallpaper.

Christmas Ring Biscuits

These look very festive indeed tied to the Christmas tree with bright green or red ribbon.

8oz (225g) plain flour	4oz (125g) icing sugar, sifted
5oz (150g) butter (not margarine), softened but not runny	1 egg (size 3), beaten
	extra milk to mix if necessary
	caster sugar for sprinkling

1 Sift flour into bowl. Rub in butter. Toss in icing sugar.
2 Mix to stiff dough with beaten egg, and a few tsp milk if necessary to hold dough together.
3 Knead briefly on floured surface until smooth, then wrap in foil and refrigerate for about 30 minutes.
4 Roll out thinly on a floured surface and cut into 30 rounds with a 2in (5cm) biscuit cutter. Remove centres with a ½in (1¼cm) cutter, then re-roll and re-cut trimmings to make required number of rings.
5 Transfer carefully to greased baking trays, brush with milk and sprinkle with sugar.
6 Bake for 12-15 minutes until pale gold, in oven set to 180°C (350°F), Gas 4. Remove from oven and cool for 3-4 minutes.
7 Transfer to wire rack and store in an airtight tin when cold, prior to packing.

Packing Arrange carefully in box lined with tissue paper. Add a roll of ribbon for threading through each and tying to the tree. Wrap in cling film, then wrap again with Christmas paper. Alternatively, wrap in fours in assorted-coloured cellophane paper and seal with sticky tape. Transfer to a sack or swag-bag (see Chapter 1) with roll of ribbon. Don't forget an instruction card, explaining that the ribbon should be threaded through biscuits and then tied carefully to the branches of the tree.

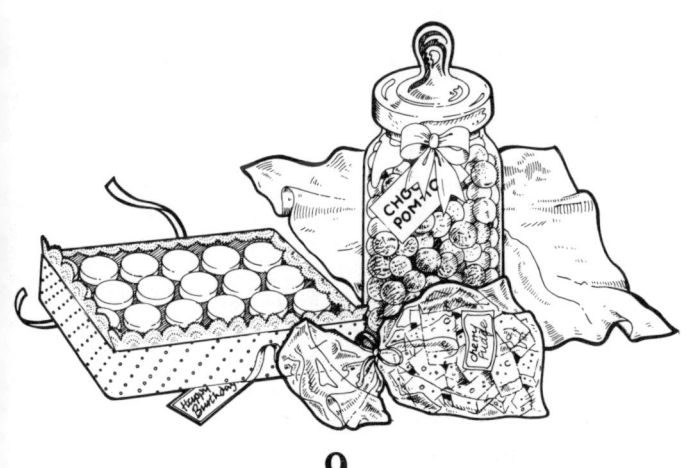

9
Confectionery

Although there is a marvellous variety of sweets and chocolates available from shops, an assorted box of home-made ones takes a lot of beating. For those who would like to start by trying out a fairly simple range, the recipes below should come in handy. For a more comprehensive selection, I suggest you look through a number of cookery books.

Walnut Cherry Fudge

An easy-to-make but deliciously creamy fudge, which looks good by itself or as part of a mixed box.

1lb (450g) granulated sugar	2oz (50g) walnuts, coarsely chopped
3 level tbsp golden syrup	
¼pt (150ml) milk	2oz (50g) glacé cherries, quartered
1 tsp vanilla essence	

1 Put sugar, syrup and milk into large pan and stir over low heat until sugar dissolves.
2 Bring to a brisk boil. Boil, stirring occasionally, for about 15 minutes or until a little of the mixture, when dropped into a cup of cold water, forms a soft ball when rolled between finger and thumb.
3 Remove from heat and cool for 10 minutes. Stir in nuts, cherries and vanilla. Beat until fudge thickens and loses its shine.

4 Spread smoothly into greased tin and cut into about 40 squares when cold. Transfer to paper sweet-cases.

Packing Pack, in single layer, in a doily-lined box. Either cover with lid if it fits, or wrap in cellophane (see Chapter 1). Alternatively, use as part of a selection.

Coffee Walnut Fudge

Make and pack as Walnut Cherry Fudge, but add 1 level tbsp instant coffee powder with the milk, and increase walnuts to 3oz (75g). Omit cherries.

Marzipan 'Potatoes'

Something in which the children can get themselves absorbed and involved.

Buy an 8oz (225g) block of marzipan and roll into 18-20 'Potatoes'. Toss in cocoa powder or drinking chocolate and put each one into a paper sweet-case.

Packing Put into a polythene bag, then pop into a homemade sack or swag-bag (see Chapter 1). Alternatively, use as part of selection.

Note: If the polythene bag is pulled tight around the 'Potatoes' inside, they will not fall out of their paper cases.

Peppermint Rounds

Good to serve after dinner with coffee, and the flavour can be varied to suit individual tastes.

1lb (450g) icing sugar	egg white from size 3 egg
2oz (50g) glucose powder	1 tbsp water
(available from chemists)	1 tsp peppermint essence

1 Sift sugar and glucose into bowl. Beat egg white and water until they just begin to foam.
2 Add to sugar and glucose. Using a fork, work together to form a stiffish paste. Turn on to surface dusted with more sifted icing sugar.
3 Knead until smooth, then roll out to about ¼in (6mm) in thickness.
4 Cut into rounds with a 1in (2.5cm) plain cutter, and

transfer to a board lined with greaseproof paper.

5 Re-roll and re-cut trimmings, then leave until set (a few hours) before transferring to paper sweet-cases. Makes about 1lb (450g).

Note: If mixture is too wet to roll, work in extra sugar; if too dry, a few tsps of water.

Packing If in paper sweet-cases, layer into a fancy box with freezer film between layers. Cover with lid or overwrap with cellophane paper. Alternatively, pack into a fancy jelly mould (glass or pottery), a fluted cake mould (see Chapter 1) or a glass or stoneware jar.

Chocolate Peppermint Creams

Make and pack as Peppermint Rounds but after cutting out, brush tops of each with melted milk or white chocolate. Leave until chocolate sets completely before moving.

Rum Rounds

Make and pack as Peppermint Rounds, but flavour with 1 or 2 tsp rum essence instead of peppermint. Colour very pale orange with edible food colouring.

Lemon Rounds

Make and pack as Peppermint Rounds, but add finely grated peel of 1 large washed-and-dried lemon to the sifted sugar and glucose. Colour pale yellow with edible food colouring.

Favourite Mocha Squares

The easiest fudge-type sweet of all, uncooked and quite delicious.

1 bar (3½oz or 100g) plain chocolate	2 heaped tsp instant coffee powder
2oz (50g) butter	3 tbsp double cream
	1lb (450g) icing sugar, sifted

1 Break up chocolate and put in basin with butter. Stand over a pan of hot water. Leave until melted, stirring once or twice.

2 Remove basin from pan and wipe sides dry. Stir in coffee powder and cream.
3 Fork in icing sugar, bit by bit, stirring until the mixture is evenly combined.
4 Spread into an 8in (20cm) buttered tin and refrigerate until firm. Cut into about 50 pieces.

Packing Transfer to paper sweet-cases and arrange, in single layer, in fancy box lined with tissue paper or doilies. Cover with lid if it fits, or wrap in coloured cellophane paper. Add a bow of ribbon.

Favourite Mocha Brazil Squares

Make and pack as Favourite Mocha Squares, adding 3oz (75g) brazil nuts just before the icing sugar.

Chocolate Pom-poms

Crisp and temptingly-flavoured, these Pom-Poms are a real winner and keep indefinitely.

1 bar (3½oz or 100g) plain chocolate	6oz (175g) digestive biscuits, finely crushed
1 tsp vanilla essence	½oz (15g) sifted icing sugar
1oz (25g) butter	½oz (15g) drinking chocolate powder

1 Break up chocolate, and put, with essence and pieces of butter, into basin standing over pan of hot water.
2 Leave until melted, stirring once or twice. Remove basin from pan and wipe sides clean.
3 Stir in crushed biscuits thoroughly, then refrigerate until mixture firms-up — about 30 minutes.
4 Form into 24 balls. Roll 12 in icing sugar, and 12 in the drinking chocolate.

Packing Transfer to paper cases and pack, in single layer, in decorative box. Top with lid if it fits, or wrap in coloured cellophane. Add a trimming of ribbon. Alternatively, layer carefully into a chunky glass jar with stopper and wrap in decorative gift paper. Tie with ribbon.

Cherry Toppers

Buy a 1lb (450g) block of marzipan and roll into 36-40

balls. Press flat (but not too flat), then top each with half a glacé cherry. Put into paper sweet-cases.

Packing   Transfer to a doily-lined box, then overwrap with red cellophane paper. Tie round with ribbon.

Chocolate Truffles

Rich and traditional, and a most elegant gift.

2 bars (each 3½oz or 100g) plain chocolate	1 tsp vanilla essence
3oz (75g) butter	8oz (225g) icing sugar, sifted
	2 tbsp double cream

Suggested coatings:
chocolate vermicelli
toasted coconut
cocoa powder
sifted icing sugar
finely chopped walnuts

1 Break up chocolate and put, with pieces of butter and essence, into basin standing over pan of hot water. Leave until melted, stirring once or twice.
2 Take basin off pan and wipe sides dry. Gradually stir in sugar and cream. Mix thoroughly. Leave in refrigerator a short time to firm-up.
3 Roll into about 30 balls then coat with any of the ingredients listed.

Packing   Transfer to paper sweet-cases and arrange, in single layer, in doily-lined and decorated box, or on a porcelain plate, either round or oval. Wrap in cling film or cellophane paper, then add a trimming or ribbon. Store in the refrigerator until the time comes for giving away.

Rum Truffles

Make and pack as Chocolate Truffles, but add 1 tbsp rum essence instead of vanilla.

Brandy Truffles

Make and pack as Chocolate Truffles, but add 1 tbsp brandy instead of vanilla.

Mocha Truffles

Make and pack as Chocolate Truffles, but add 1 tbsp very strong coffee instead of vanilla.

10
Food Hampers, Fruit and Nuts

Very costly to buy, food hampers and fruit packs can be much more economically produced at home – and make a change from flowers or pot plants. All you need by way of investment is a handled basket or small wicker picnic-basket, lots of tissue paper and a selection of tins and packets or fruit. As hampers are usually a Christmas treat, the foods I have chosen are designed for that, but of course you can vary them for any time of year.

Hamper 1: Connoisseur

Fill a tissue-lined basket with the following: can of liver pâté, whole Stilton cheese or lidded pottery jar containing cheese, packet of Bath Oliver biscuits, bottle of port, box of marrons glacés or liqueur chocolates and a tin of butter shortbreads. Wrap in cellophane paper, and attach a gift card, a bow of ribbon and a sprig of holly or mistletoe.

Hamper 2: Family

Fill a tissue-lined hamper with a Christmas pudding in a basin ready for steaming, or an iced Christmas cake with: can of ham, can of boned chicken, can of tongue, jar of olives, jar of gherkins, jar of mincemeat for making

Mince Pies, miniature bottle of brandy, pot of Rum or Brandy Butter (or one of each), tin of assorted biscuits, box of mixed glacé fruits, box of dates, box of figs, bag of mixed nuts in shells, baby farmhouse Cheddar cheese, packet of semi-sweet biscuits and a bottle of medium sherry. Scatter a few brightly-wrapped chocolates, such as 'Roses' or 'Quality Street', then wrap hamper completely in cellophane paper.

Hamper 3: Children

Fill a tissue-lined hamper or basket with 2 bottles of fruit squash, about 6 bright-red apples, packets of Twiglets, salted peanuts and crisps, a large tube of Smarties, a large bar of milk chocolate, and a packet of chocolate biscuits. Tuck in some baby crackers and Christmas novelties, then wrap completely in cellophane.

Hamper 4: Solo

People who live alone are often appreciative of a hamper of small items which can be eaten at once without leftovers. Below are just a few suggestions.

Line a small food hamper or basket with tissue paper. Add: a can of tomato or oxtail soup, a small can of red salmon, a small can of luncheon meat, a small Christmas pudding in basin ready for steaming, 2 Mince Pies, a small pot of Rum or Brandy Butter, 2 small cans of fruits such as peaches and cherries, a small box of mixed chocolates, a jar of instant coffee powder, 2 oranges, 1 dessert pear, 2 red apples, 2 bananas, a packet of cream crackers and a box of assorted cheesy biscuits.

Exotic Basket

Choose a medium-sized basket, line with coloured tissue paper and make the focal point a large pineapple with a perfect crown of leaves. Surround with oranges, then add 2 small melons, 4 kiwi fruit and/or 12 lychees, 2 mangoes or 2 paw-paws, 4 passion fruit and clusters of grapes. Gently push tissue paper between fruits to save bruising, and dot here and there with unshelled nuts and firm plums.

Wrap in cellophane paper and finish with a large bow of green ribbon.

Mixed Fruit Hamper

Treat as the Exotic Basket, but make the focal point oranges and grapefruits. Add apples, pears, lemons and a bunch of slightly under-ripe bananas. Vary according to taste and season.

Tropical Nut Mix

2oz (50g) unsalted peanuts	1oz (25g) coarsely flaked coconut
1oz (25g) dried banana flakes	2oz (50g) seedless raisins
	½oz (15g) pine nuts

Mix all ingredients together and transfer to a glass jar with stopper.

Packing Wrap in fancy gift paper and tie round with ribbon or braid.

Garlic Almonds

3oz (75g) butter	12oz (350g) blanched almonds
1 garlic clove, peeled and halved	salt to taste
2 tsp salad oil	paprika

1 Heat butter in pan with garlic and oil. Keep heat low to prevent burning. Add nuts.
2 Increase heat slightly and fry until almonds are a warm golden-brown.
3 Remove from pan with spoon and drain on crumpled kitchen paper. Toss, while still hot, with salt to taste and paprika. Leave until cold before packing.

Packing As Tropical Mix.

Curried Brazils

6oz (175g) brazil nuts	salt to taste
2oz (50g) butter	about 4 rounded tsp mild curry powder
2 tsp salad oil	

1 Slice brazils thickly and fry in butter and oil until pale gold.
2 Remove from pan and drain on crumpled kitchen paper. Toss in salt and curry powder to taste.

Packing As Tropical Mix.